London is a test bed for bet
magnet for freethinkers w
sorts of weird and wonder
best museums, art gallerie
notch architects, chefs, fas
and artists whose work an
cultures, both in the West

C000023252

CITIx60: London explores the British capital in five aspects, cover-
ing architecture, art spaces, shops and markets, eating and enter-
tainments. With expert advice from 60 stars of London's creative
scene, this book guides you to the real attractions of the city for an
authentic taste of London life.

Contents

Before You Go

BASIC INFO

Currency
Pound Sterling (GBP/£)
Exchange rate: £1 : S1.3 : €1.14

Time zone
GMT +0
DST +1

DST begins at 0100 (local time) on the last Sunday of March and ends at 0100 (local time) on the last Sunday of October.

Dialling
International calling: +44
Citywide: (0)20*

*Dial (0) for calls made within UK.

Weather (average temperature range)
Spring (Mar–May): 7–15°C / 45–59°F
Summer (Jun–Sep): 13–22°C / 55–72°F
Autumn (Oct–Nov): 8–15°C / 46–59°F
Winter (Dec–Feb): 2–10°C / 36–50°F

USEFUL WEBSITES

Transport for London
www.tfl.gov.uk

Pocket WIFI
Tep
www.tepwireless.com

EMERGENCY CALLS

Ambulance, fire or police (24hrs)
999 or 112

Non-life-threatening emergencies
111

Embassies
China   +44 (0)20 7299 4049
Japan   +44 (0)20 7465 6500
France   +44 (0)20 7073 1000
Germany   +44 (0)20 7824 1300
US   +44 (0)20 7499 9000

AIRPORT EXPRESS TRANSFER

Heathrow <–> Paddington (Heathrow Express)
Trains / Journey: every 15 mins / 15 mins
From Heathrow (T2&3): 0512–2348 (M–Sa), 0623–2353 (Su)
From Paddington: 0510–2325 (M–Sa), 0610–2325 (Su)
One-way: £22/25, Return: £37 (£5.50 online booking discount)
www.heathrowexpress.com

Gatwick <–> Victoria Station (Gatwick Express)
Trains / Journey: every 15 mins / 30 mins
From Gatwick: 0536–2300
From Victoria: 0551–2320 (M–F, Su), 0545– (Sa)
One-way: £17.80, Return: £24.30–31.60 (10% online booking discount)
www.gatwickexpress.com

Train frequency and timetable vary at early and late hours, especially on Sundays.

PUBLIC TRANSPORT IN LONDON

Tube
Overground
National rail
Santander Bikes
Thames Clipper
Bus (Oyster payment only)
Taxi

Means of Payment
Oyster card
Cash

Bus and tram daily price cap applies to Oyster card users. Under 11s travel free.

PUBLIC (BANK) HOLIDAYS

January	1 New Year's Day
April	Good Friday, Easter Monday
May	Early May & Spring bank holiday (1st & last Mon)
August	Summer bank holiday (Last Mon)
December	25 Christmas Day, 26 Boxing Day

If a bank holiday falls on a weekend, the following weekday becomes a 'substitute' day. Most public services suspend on Dec 25.

FESTIVALS / EVENTS

February
London Fashion Week (Also in September)
www.londonfashionweek.co.uk

May
Museums at Night (Also in October)
museumsatnight.org.uk

June
Royal Academy of Arts
Summer Exhibition (Through to August)
www.royalacademy.org.uk
Trooping the Colour
www.trooping-the-colour.co.uk
ArchFilmFest London (Next one in 2019)
archfilmfest.uk
Here London by It's Nice That
www.itsnicethat.com

July
Summer Series at Sommerset House
www.somersethouse.org.uk
Love Box
loveboxfestival.com

August
Great British Beer Festival
gbbf.org.uk

September
The London Design Festival
www.londondesignfestival.com
Open House London
www.openhouselondon.org.uk
100% Design
www.100percentdesign.co.uk

October
Frieze Art Fair
www.friezelondon.com

Event days may vary by year. Please check for updates online.

UNUSUAL OUTINGS

Alternative London
www.alternativeldn.com

Artangel / Janet Cardiff: The Missing Voice
www.artangel.org.uk
(Note: Please start from Whitechapel Gallery which has absorbed the Library where the original experience began. Take the entrance closest to Osborn Street/Brick Lane.)

Art Licks
www.artlicks.com

First Thurdays
whitechapelgallery.org/first-thursdays

HintHunt
hinthunt.co.uk

The Northern Heights / Parkland Walk
www.urban75.org/london/alexandra.html

SMARTPHONE APP

Routeing & navigation
Citymapper
Busmapper (iOS only)
Live London Bus Tracker (Andriod only)

Burger hunt
Burgerapp

REGULAR EXPENSES

Newspaper
£1-3

Domestic / International mail (postcard)
56p / £1.17

Gratuities
Diners: optional £1-2 or 12.5% by policy
Hotels: £2 for the porter, £2 daily for cleaners
Licensed taxis: round up the fare to the nearest £1 or £2-5 for assistance with luggage.

Count to 10

What makes London so special?

Illustrations by Guillaume Kashima aka Funny Fun

London is a world cultural capital full of characters. The city's stories are told through its accumulation of architectural excellence, rich history and heritage, a diverse taste for music and art, and an impressive, flourishing food culture. Whether you are on a one-day stopover or a week-long stay, see what London creatives consider essential to see, taste, read and take home from your trip.

1

Museums & Galleries

Tate Modern & Tate Britain
www.tate.org.uk

Victoria and Albert Museum
www.vam.ac.uk

The British Museum
www.britishmuseum.org

Design Museum
designmuseum.org

The National Gallery
www.nationalgallery.org.uk

Royal Academy of Arts
www.royalacademy.org.uk

Somerset House
www.somersethouse.org.uk

2

Architecture

30 St Mary Axe
by Sir Norman Foster,
Ken Shuttleworth

The Shard (#7)
by Renzo Piano

City Hall
by Sir Norman Foster

Millennium Bridge
by Arup, Foster and Partners &
Sir Anthony Caro

The Barbican (#6)
by Chamberlin, Powell & Bon

Lloyd's Building
by Richard Rogers

Trellick Tower
by Ernő Goldfinger

3

Nourishment

Pie, mash and liquor
Manzes
76 High St., E17 7LD

Jellied eels
F. Cooke
9 Broadway Market, E8 4PH

Roast beef
Simpson's in the Strand
www.simpsonsinthestrand.co.uk

Fish & Chips
The Rock & Sole Plaice
rockandsoleplaice.com

Salad & Bakery
Ottolenghi
www.ottolenghi.co.uk

Doughnuts
St. John Bar & Restaurant (#47)
www.stjohngroup.uk.com

4

Mementos

Handmade screwdriver
Labour and Wait
www.labourandwait.co.uk

Modish hats
Lock & Co.
www.lockhatters.co.uk

Vintage-inspired Menswear
De Rien
www.derien.co.uk

Rare pickles, preserves & teas
Fortnum & Mason
www.fortnumandmason.com

Homemade Jam
London Borough of Jam
londonboroughofjam.tumblr.com

SUBWAY GALLERY
badge or sticker
SUBWAY GALLERY
www.subwaygallery.com

5

Independent Bookseller

Graphic arts publishing house
NoBrow Press (Web shop only)
www.nobrow.net

**Reprints of neglected classics
by mid-1920 women authors**
Persephone Books
www.persephonebooks.co.uk

**Author-curated options
& handicrafts**
Libreria, *libreria.io*

**Art, photography, cultural
theory & indie publications**
Donlon Books, *donlonbooks.com*

**Limited edition books, small
press monographs & journals**
Ti Pi Tin (#25)

Design books & gifts
Magma Books (#27)

6

Street Markets

Borough Market
www.boroughmarket.org.uk

Camden Market
camdenmarket.com

Brick Lane Market
www.visitbricklane.org

Portobello Road Market
www.portobelloroad.co.uk

Broadway Market
www.broadwaymarket.co.uk

**Columbia Road
Flower Market (#36)**
www.columbiaroad.info

7

Leisure

Fly a kite or swim in the pond
Hampstead Heath

Watch Trooping the Colour
Buckingham Palace

See the city from the Thames
www.thamesclippers.com

Watch people in a café
Portobello Road

**Explore side streets on a
Santander Bike**
Santander Cycles (app)

**Find an old London Bus
to ride on**
Route no. 9 and 15

8

Locally Crafted Beer

The Jerusalem Tavern
*www.stpetersbrewery.co.uk/
london-pub*

Camden Town Brewery
www.camdentownbrewery.com

The Dove
dovehammersmith.co.uk

The Royal Oak
www.royaloaklondon.com

Happiness Forgets
www.happinessforgets.com

The Bermondsey Beer Mile
*From Southwark Brewing
Company to Fourpure Brewery*

9

Live Gigs & Performance Art

O2 Brixton Academy
*academymusicgroup.com/
o2academybrixton*

The Troubadour
troubadourlondon.com

VFD
vfdalston.com

Bloc.
blocweekend.com

Kentish Town
Kentish Town, NW5

10

Tattoos

Flamin' Eight
www.flamineight.co.uk

The Family Business
thefamilybusinesstattoo.com

Good Times
goodtimestattoo.co.uk

Hammersmith Tattoo
hammersmithtattoo.co.uk

Prick
www.henryhate.com

Shall Adore Tattoo
www.shalladoretattoo.com

Icon Index

 Opening hours   Admission

 Address   Facebook

Contact   **URL** Website

Remarks

 Scan QR codes to access Google Maps and discover the area around each destination. Internet connection required.

60x60

60 Local Creatives x 60 Hotspots

From vast cityscapes to the tiniest glimpses of everyday exchanges, there's always something to provoke your imagination. 60X60 points you to 60 haunts where 60 arbiters of taste cut their teeth.

Landmarks & Architecture SPOTS · 01 – 12 📍

London's skyline takes in a variety of architectural styles in distinctive shapes. But it's not at all a concrete jungle. It's customary to bide your time at one of the many parks.

Cultural & Art Spaces SPOTS · 13 – 24 📍

The city's cultural scene is thriving with the world's best museums, galleries and creative projects. Turning up at the shows is the best way to learn the noteworthy names.

Markets & Shops SPOTS · 25 – 36 📍

Get ready for eye-opening discoveries as London markets and shops stock everything one could possibly desire, from vintage to designer, and cheap eats to art.

Restaurants & Cafés SPOTS · 37 – 48 📍

Be blessed with gastronomic artistry. Among fresh catches from the sea, grilled meat and local produce, there are also delicate cakes to fill your tummy from day to night.

Nightlife SPOTS · 49 – 60 📍

Live gigs, open cinema and swing dances – there is always too much to do in one night. Be sure to check schedules and plan well to maximise your night.

Landmarks & Architecture

Historic sites, iconic buildings and popular green spaces

London is a centuries-spanning mix of architectural structures and styles. Dominated by 18-19th century Georgian and Victorian buildings that emerged after the Great Fire in 1666 and progressing with 20th century Brutalism, best exemplified in the design of The Barbican (#6) and Bowellism (e.g. Lloyd's building by Richard Rogers), followed by modern constructions like 30 St Mary Axe or the City Hall by Sir Norman Foster, this urban landscape only grows more exciting as time goes by. Aside from the sites mentioned in this section, architecture enthusiasts should not overlook the British Museum's Great Court (Foster+Partners). To get a glimpse of London's drastically changing skyline, walk along the River Thames or hop on the highly-recommended Thames Clipper. Other iconic structures, including Trellick Tower (Ernő Goldfinger), London Zoo's Penguin Pool (Tecton Group) and Snowden Aviary (Cedric Price), never disappoint. Linking the outstanding architecture are bountiful parks that make up a distinctive feature of London and form an essential part of local recreational life. Visit at least one Royal Park or try to swim in one of Hampstead Heath's ponds to really cut to the heart of London at leisure.

Form
Creative agency

Founded by Paul West and Paula Benson in 1991, Form is now a team of six. Their background lies predominantly in the music industry but now extends to other sectors too.

The Monument 015

tokyoplastic
Multimedia creative agency

We are Sam Lanyon Jones and Andrew Cope. We have been creating animation, vinyl collectables and web-based experiences from our London studio for the past ten years.

Foundry Studio
Creative agency

Foundry combines different skills and crafts, and brings together talented individuals across diverse disciplines to produce work that is original and distinctive.

Southbank Centre 014

Battersea Power Station 016

Oscar Bolton Green
Graphic artist

I graduated from Camberwell College of Arts in 2010 and have been creating designs for books, advertising, animations and exhibitions since. My clients include Nike and MTV.

St. Paul's Cathedral 018

Richard Scott
Founder, Surface Architects

I am an architect, teaching and experimenting in the UK and abroad. Having set up Surface in 1999, I work independently with architects, designers, educators and entrepreneurs.

Alan Dye
Creative director, NB

I co-own NB Studio with Nick Finney. We are an independent branding and communication studio. We love design and believe in the power of a good idea.

Holland Park 017

The Barbican 019

James Joyce
Graphic artist

I am an artist and designer living and working in London. My studio is based in Shoreditch, East London.

Primrose Hill
023

Raoul Shah
Founder, Exposure

CEO and creative director of Exposure, a communications agency with offices in London, New York and Tokyo. We've been making brands culturally relevant since 1993.

Von
Artist

Von is behind award winning studio HelloVon and online store ShopVon through which I release fine art limited editions and originals.

The
Shard
022

Highgate
Cemetery
024

Alida Rosie Sayer
Graphic designer & artist

I've been living in London since 2009. My creative practice encompasses a wide range of disciplines, but primarily focuses on the intersection of language, form and experience.

Postman's
Park
026

Dan Tobin Smith
Photographer

Originally from Kent, I've been based in London since I was two. I work on editorial and commercials, and specialise in larger still life installations.

Supermundane
Graphic artist & writer

I'm an artist, typographer, writer, I'm Rob Lowe. My abstract drawings have been exhibited and published world-wide. I'm also the art director of food journal, *Fire & Knives*.

The
Goldfinger
House
025

The Crystal
Palace
Dinosaurs
027

1 Southbank Centre

Map C, P.104

Southbank Centre's bold, blockish Modern-ist compound comprises Royal Festival Hall (RFH) – a lasting legacy of the 1951 Festival of Britain – as well as Queen Elizabeth Hall (QEH), Purcell Room, the Hayward Gallery (HG) and the Saison Poetry Library. The 21-acre site is often enlivened with street musicians, skateboard-ers and other diverse outdoor performers, just waiting to be discovered. The Hayward has an amazing rolling art exhibition programme that typically features avant-garde installations by the world's leading contemporary artists.

🕐 RFH: 1000–2300 daily
🏠 Belvedere Rd., SE1 8XX
📞 +44 (0)20 3879 9555
🔗 www.southbankcentre.co.uk
🖉 QEH & HG are due to reopen in 2018

"Walk from Westminster Bridge to the Millennium Bridge at night and see the incredible multicultural delights of London."

– Form

2 The Monument
Map C, P.105

The Great Fire of London in 1666 gutted most of the walled City of London over four days, including St. Paul's Cathedral. The fire began in a baker's house on nearby Pudding Lane, 202 feet from the flame-topped Monument's current location, which is the reason for the stone column's precise height. The west side of its base displays a bas relief by Caius Gabriel Cibber depicting Charles II directing the city's restoration with his brother James II.

🕐 Daily: 0930–1800 (Apr–Sep), –1730 (Oct–Mar)
💲 £4.50/3/2.30
🏠 Fish Street Hill, EC3R 8AH
🔗 www.themonument.info
✐ Cash only

"There are more steps than Covent Garden tube, and the spiral staircase gets narrower as you progress to the top – not something vertigo sufferers would enjoy."

– Foundry Studio

3 Battersea Power Station
Map K, P.110

An icon of Art Deco, industrial architecture and Europe's largest brick building, the cathedral-style coal-fired boiler house was constructed in two phases punctuated by WWII. This explains the Italian marble, polished parquet floorings and wrought-iron staircases in A Station's control room, and the stainless steel fittings in B Station, east of A. The Grade II listed building has been a staple symbol of London's pop culture, appearing on a Pink Floyd album, a Batman movie and has hosted numerous fashion shows. Until it opens anew in 2019, work is underway to transform the surrounding areas into a bright new community.

🏠 *188 Kirtling St., SW8 5BN*
URL *www.batterseapowerstation.co.uk*

"A great view of the station can be seen from any of the trains from London Victoria and from the boat towards Kew Gardens from Westminster Pier."

– tokyoplastic

4 Holland Park
Map L, P.110

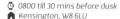

Originally the grounds of Cope Castle, a 17th-century Jacobean mansion later renamed Holland House, Holland Park opened to the public in 1952. Characterised by a semi-wild woodland area, the park also features Kyoto Garden, built in celebration of London's 1992 Japan Festival, an orangery, and a population of squirrels and peacocks. Walk from High Street Kensington Station to explore the affluent area's Victorian townhouses, the Design Museum by John Pawson and OMA, and the elaborate Orientalist interiors of Lord Leighton's former house at 12 Holland Park Road.

🕐 *0800 till 30 mins before dusk*
📍 *Kensington, W8 6LU*

"It's my favourite park in London. A great place to relax and have a coffee. Get an ice-cream and have a walk round Kyoto Garden."

– Oscar Bolton Green

5 St. Paul's Cathedral

Map C, P.104

The present cathedral dedicated to Paul the Apostle is at least the fourth to have stood on the site. Designed in English Baroque style by Sir Christopher Wren (1632–1723) after its predecessor was destroyed in the Great Fire, St. Paul's has became the second largest church building with nested domes in the UK. Experience the unique ethereal acoustics in The Whispering Gallery – the first dome you'll reach, as well as panoramic views of London from The Golden Gallery around the highest point of the outer dome. Be sure to check out the crypt where Wren now rests.

🕐 M-Sa: 0830–1630 (sightseeing), Su: worship only
💲 £18/16/8 🏠 St. Paul's Churchyard, EC4M 8AD
🔗 www.stpauls.co.uk 📞 +44 (0)20 7246 8350
📎 Stone & Golden Gallery will be closed from September 11 through November 10, 2017.

"Because it's over 300 years old and is such a beautiful and inspiring building. It says London to me."

– Alan Dye, NB

6 The Barbican
Map C, P.105

Designed by Chamberlin, Powell & Bon in 1954 but not completed until the 1980s, the Barbican Complex is a Grade II listed Brutalist masterpiece featuring the Barbican Arts Centre – Europe's largest performing arts centre – and the Barbican Estate, a residential complex comprised of 13 terrace blocks and three towers, connected by above-ground walkways known as High Walks. Look for the hidden indoor tropical oasis on the main building's third floor, which is populated by finches, quails, exotic fish and over 2,000 species of tropical plants and trees.

🕐 0900–2300 (M–Sa), 1100– (Su), 1200– (P.H.),
Conservatory: 1200-1700 (Su & P.H.)
🏠 Silk St., EC2Y 8DS
📞 +44 (0)20 7638 4141
URL www.barbican.org.uk

"Go very early to performances in order to soak up the atmosphere and find other things to do. "

– Richard Scott, Surface Architects

7 The Shard
Map C, P.105

Love or hate The Shard, one of London's most fiercely debated new works, most everyone agrees the glass-clad pyramid designed by Renzo Piano provides the mind visual stimuli. The 87-floor building houses the Shangri-La hotel, and viewing floors here are at twice the height of anywhere else in the city, providing one exclusive 360° view. Standing at approximately 310 metres high, the Shard is the tallest building in the UK as of 2017.

🏠 32 London Bridge St., SE1 9SG 🔲 the-shard.com
🎟 The View from The Shard: Apr–Oct: 1000–2200 (Su–F), –2115 (Sa), Nov–Mar: 1000–1900 (Su–W), –2200 (Th–Sa), £24.95–30.95, 15% online booking discount, Last entry is one hour before closing, www.theviewfromtheshard.com

"Go to The View at the top of the tower. It's almost twice the height of any other viewing platform in London."

– James Joyce

8 Primrose Hill

Map H, P.109

As well as one of the town's most exclusive and upscale residential neighbourhoods, Primrose Hill is ideal for a quick getaway. Take a summer picnic or simply read and relax overlooking London's famous skyline. The grassy hillside is just north of Regent's Park, whose London Zoo boasts 700 animal species and ten listed structures, including the Modernist Penguin Pool by Tecton Group and the Snowden Aviary by Cedric Price.

🕐 *0500 till dusk daily*
📍 *Primrose Hill, NW1 4NR*
📞 *+44 (0)30 0061 2300*

"Aim to be at the top before sunset. There's a ton of great pubs (The Landsdowne) and restaurants (Lemonia) to check out in the village afterwards."

– Raoul Shah, Exposure

9 Highgate Cemetery
Map D, P.106

Designated Grade I and run by The Friends of Highgate Cemetery Trust, Highgate Cemetery occupies a spectacular south-facing hillside area featuring a vast mix of woodland interspersed with Victorian graves. Egyptian Avenue and Circle of Lebanon mark entry to the original site, opened in 1839, and now referred to as the West Cemetery. Highgate's notable residents include James Bunstone Bunning, the architect who oversaw cemetery planning on the West side; and Malcolm McLaren, Patrick Caulfield and Karl Marx at its East side extension.

🕐 💲 *East: 1000–1700 (M–F), 1100– (Sa–Su & P.H.), Nov–Feb: closes at 1600, £4, Guided tour: 1400 (Sa), £8/4 (incl. entry); West: by guided tour only, 8+, 1345 (M–F, online booking only), 1100–1600 (Sa–Su & P.H., tickets sold on site from 10.45am, Nov–Feb: last tour leaves at 1500), £12/6 (incl. entry to East)*
🏠 *Swain's Ln., N6 6PJ* 📞 *+44 (0)20 8340 1834*
URL *www.highgatecemetery.org*

"A hidden gem in North London's Highgate. Well worth the visit, somewhere you can loose all sense of time."

– Von

10 The Goldfinger House
Map O, P.111

🕐 *March though October: By guided tour only: 1100-1400, Self-guided viewing: 1500-1700 (W–Su & P.H. Mondays)*
💲 *£6.50/3.25* 🏠 *2 Willow Rd., NW3 1TH*
🔗 *www.nationaltrust.org.uk/2-willow-road*

Hungarian-born Ernő Goldfinger (1902-87) was one of the foremost architects in the Brutalist and Modernist movements. He designed and built this small yet perfectly formed gem of iconic Modernist architecture with his wife Ursula in 1939. The house became a key location for the left wing idealist Hampstead intellectual creative community that thrived during the 1930s and 40s, with neighbours, including Henry Moore, Barbara Hepworth and Ben Nicholson, also appearing in the Goldfinger modern art collections displayed throughout the house.

"Ask the exceptionally enthusiastic volunteers lots of questions, they know everything there is to know!"

– Alida Rosie Sayer

11 Postman's Park
Map C, P.104

Named Postman's Park because it neighbours the old General Post Office, this hidden green features a Wall of Heroes erected in 1900 to honour heroic civilians. One such, Alice Ayers, was a nursemaid honoured after she saved her tiny wards but died herself in a house fire, and whose name is now immortalised in the film *Closer* (2004), as the character played by Natalie Portman. The park is built on former burial grounds, closed under the Burial Act of 1851 for Public Health, when the grounds became over-burdened by bodies.

🕐 *0800 till dusk daily*
📍 *St. Martin's Le-Grand, Little Britain & King Edward St., EC1A 7BT*

"Nice place to have lunch in the summer."
– Dan Tobin Smith

12 The Crystal Palace Dinosaurs
Map P, P.111

These monstrous animal models were the Victorian impression of the Jurassic age, and are the oldest dinosaur sculptures in the world. Created mostly on speculation in the 1850s, predating Charles Darwin's *The Origin of Species* (1859), the prehistoric theme park complemented the reopening of Crystal Palace, home to The Great Exhibition before its destruction by fire in 1936. Architectural highlights include the National Sports Centre, Concert Bowl and a fan-vaulted subway that led to the now disused old High Level Station.

🕑 *0730 till dusk daily*
🏠 *Thicket Rd, SE19 2GA*
🔗 *www.crystalpalacepark.org.uk*
🎧 *Free audio guide (Darwin & the Dinosaurs audio trail): www.audiotrails.co.uk/dinosaurs*

> *"It's so old that most of the sculptures are wrong. Take a walk around and try to imagine it when the huge Crystal Palace still stood overlooking the park."*
>
> – Supermundane aka Rob Lowe

Cultural & Art Spaces

Museums, art galleries and creative projects

London is known for its high concentration of world-class museums and art galleries. From historic houses to museums of natural history, medicine or art, many museums demonstrate excellent depth and dimension of the objects they conserve and the inspiring exhibitions they curate. Art galleries too have been aggressively discovering new perspectives, talents and works, initiating innovative cultural projects or artistic collaborations with artists and architects. Seeing a new force of gallerists entering the scene, from backgrounds as varied as theatre, architecture and the fashion industry, new works constantly ask the viewer to reslant their expectations. Whether arising as commercial, social enterprise or as extensions of existing projects, a continual stream of arousing programmes engages the urban community, with frequent opportunities for social interactions and cultural exchange. As often as not, the architectural approach and story behind the buildings or sites they lodge in add significance to the content on display.

V&A Museum of Childhood, P.038

David Saunders
Fashion designer, David David

Creative director of David David, a brand that creates beautifully printed products. Clothes, furniture and original art are all marked by large splashes of colour and geometric patterns.

Kate
MacGarry
032

Horniman
Museum &
Gardens
033

Ian Wright
Artist

London born and bred, I live and work as an artist and illustrator in both London and New York.

Madame Peripetie
Fashion photographer

My name is Madame Peripetie and I am an image-maker, photographer and character designer living and working between Germany and London.

Serpentine
Galleries
034

Sawdust
Design collective

We are Rob Gonzalez and Jonathan Quainton. We do custom typography, identity and art direction across music, art & culture, fashion, corporate and advertising sectors.

Bold
Tendencies
037

Barney Beech
Co-founder, Burgess & Beech

Previously of THIS IS Studio, Barney Beech co-directs multidisciplinary practice Burgess & Beech with Dougal Burgess. Beech is a father of three.

Marta Długołęcka
Illustration artist, Kissi Kissi

Originally from Warsaw, I am a Kingston University graduate with an MA degree from the Royal College of Art. My work mixes digital magic with a love for crafts and model making.

The Old
Truman
Brewery
036

V&A
Museum of
Childhood
038

Nick Knight
Founder, SHOWstudio

I establish and direct SHOWstudio on a manifesto of collaboration and transparency of process. I explore the possibilities of fashion film and photography in my own work.

SHOWstudio
040

Chrysostomos Naselos
Co-founder, Company

I'm design director of design studio, Company, and enjoy the small, simple and funny things in life with a bit of zing. Many times I wander aimlessly around the city, taking it all in.

White Cubicle Toilet Gallery
043

Raven Row
041

John Gilsenan
Founder, IWANT

I'm creative director and owner of design agency IWANT. Born, raised, schooled and lived in London all of my life apart from a brief spell living in the Czech Republic.

Hunterian Museum
044

Jane Bowler
Fashion designer

A lover of colour, plastic and creating fun fashion!

Build
Graphic design collective

Led by Michael Place and Nicky Place, Build produces modern graphic solutions for clients such as Virgin America, Made. com, Getty Images and events both in the UK and abroad.

Dennis, Severs' House
042

brose~fogale
Industrial design collective

We are Matteo Fogale and Joscha Brose. We stress the use of honest and premium materials, functionality and longevity in bespoke furniture and product design.

Rio Cinema
045

13 Kate MacGarry

Map F, P.107

Escape the crowds and take a turn to this clean contemporary art space inside a typical Georgian building in London. Since its opening in 2002, Kate MacGarry has put its artists forefront in complete trust, lending its beautiful white cube space to some fantastic young artists on the scene who elicit exciting conversations over humanity, the state of being and so on through surprising work. The gallery has a special interest in abstraction and represents diverse artists, including Goshka Macuga and Ben Rivers.

🕐 1200-1800 (W-Sa & by appointment)
🏠 27 Old Nichol St., E2 7HR
📞 +44 (0)20 7613 0515
🔗 www.katemacgarry.com

"Try go see some of Luke Rudolf's work."

– David Saunders, David David

14 Horniman Museum & Gardens

Map N, P.111

Established by wealthy tea trader Frederick Horniman, in 1901, to showcase his private collections. With 350,000 objects including extensive natural history specimens and 1600 musical instruments collected from his frequent trips to far-flung destinations in the East and the West, much can be examined up-close, and some even tinkered with. The Horniman also houses an impressive aquarium. The 16 acres of historic gardens around the museum present an additional living collection with medicinal plants, small animal enclosure and London's oldest Nature Trail.

🕐 1030-1730 daily, Garden: 0715 till dusk (M-Sa), 0800- (Su & P.H.)
🏠 100 London Rd., SE23 3PQ
📞 +44 (0)20 8699 1872
🔗 www.horniman.ac.uk

"I've always particularly enjoyed visiting Horniman Museum, Pride of South London! Look out for the Walrus!"

– Ian Wright

15 Serpentine Galleries

Housed in a 1934 tea pavilion, this popular gallery shows modern and contemporary art and is endowed with enormous green open space. A highlight is their summer pavilion which commissions high profile architects like Herzog & de Meuron and artist Ai Weiwei. The Serpentine Sackler Gallery opened in 2013 in a 208-year old Grade II listed former gunpowder depot is Zaha Hadid Architects' first permanent structure in central London. Koenig Books at the gallery is not to be missed.

🕐 1000–1800 (Tu–Su)
🏠 Kensington Gardens, W2 3XA
📞 +44 (0)20 7402 6075
🔗 www.serpentinegalleries.org
📎 Galleries may be closed between shows.

"It has the most ambitious architectural programme of its kind worldwide. Definitely worth visiting!"
– Madame Peripetie

On facing page: Serpentine Gallery exterior by John Offenbach / On this page, clockwise: 1-2, 4 photos courtesy of Serpentine Sackler Gallery ©2013 Luke Hayes; 3 The Royal Parks' Magazine Building, to be transformed to The Serpentine Sackler Gallery, Kensington Gardens, London, Photo: John Offenbach, ©The Royal Parks and Serpentine Gallery

16 The Old Truman Brewery
Map C, P.105

Formerly the Black Eagle Brewery, London's largest beer factory in the mid-17th century, this red-brick warehouse district underwent a 15-year regeneration programme to re-emerge as a vibrant arts and media quarter. Home to creative businesses, independent shops, galleries and restaurants with live music and performance frequently offered at night. Events at Truman include the annual Free Range Art & Design show and Fashion East, where young designers present catwalk collections for London Fashion Week.

🕐 *Opening hours vary with shops & events*
🏠 *91 Brick Ln., E1 6QL*
📞 *+44 (0)20 7770 6000*
URL *www.trumanbrewery.com*

"Very creative part of London. They often hold galleries and private views to look out for."
– Sawdust

Hannah Barry Gallery's annual summer show brings new people, international art and good vibes to this unexpected spot. Since 2007, this wonderfully original project has reinvigorated the former disused Peckham Rye Carpark, and collaborates with young talents on site-specific projects across sculpture, film, dance and music. Frank Café, that runs the rooftop kitchen, is Bold Tendencies' very first architectural commission. The resident Multi-Story Orchestra, its another partner, performs extraordinary live concerts, occasionally with local schools and community groups.

🕐 May 19-Sep 30 (2017): 1700-2300 (Tu-Th), 1400- (F), 1100- (Sa & Su)
🏠 7-10/F, Peckham Rye Carpark, 95A Rye Ln., SE15 4TG
URL www.boldtendencies.com

"Start in Brixton, have lunch in one of the many restaurants at the market. Also head over to South London Gallery on Peckham Road."

– Barney Beech, Burgess & Beech

 V&A Museum of Childhood
Map I, P.109

Let loose your inner child adventuring into the
UK's largest childhood-themed national collection orbiting artworks and artefacts. Housed
in a Grade II listed brick building, the division
of the famous Victoria and Albert Museum is
a wonderland of designed toys and objects
spanning from the 1600s up to today. As well
as rare hand-crafted objects, dolls' houses,
games and analogue toys, the museum has
an impressive archive looking into British toy
making and children's fashion across four
galleries. Museum shop sells equally endearing
toys and crafts.

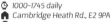

🕙 1000-1745 daily
🏠 Cambridge Heath Rd., E2 9PA
📞 +44 (0)20 8983 5200
URL www.vam.ac.uk/moc

"*This isn't a quick stop so give yourself at least couple
of hours there because there's loads to see and
you're likely to loose yourself in memories.*"
– Marta Długołęcka, Kissi Kissi

Year 6 Girl
Dirty Troll
London Fringe 1998

19 SHOWstudio
Map J, P.110

SHOWstudio remains at the forefront of the art and fashion scene. Headed and founded by Nick Knight in 2000, the website pioneered fashion film, broadcasting live from fashion shoots and initiated ground-breaking projects with influential figures such as Yohji Yamamoto, John Galliano, Alexander McQueen, Kate Moss, Lady Gaga and Björk. Its shop is an exciting gallery and shop where exhibitions revolve to present extraordinary artefacts curated by SHOWstudio around a simple theme. Recent featured artists were Iris van Herpen and Nick Knight himself.

🕐 1030-1800 (M-F)
🏠 22D Ebury St., SW1W 0LU
📞 +44 (0)20 7235 7680
URL shop.showstudio.com

"Visit showstudio.com for a taster, swing by the shop to see it in the flesh."
– Nick Knight, SHOWstudio

20 Raven Row
Map C, P.105

Originally a weapons practice ground, the Raven Row space was built in 1754 with some of the finest surviving examples of Rococo design. Now reborn as a non-profit contemporary art and exhibition space funded and programmed by Alex Sainsbury, the three-storey Georgian townhouse zeros in on work by established international artists or those from the recent past. The grounds link with a 1970s office space, while upper floors are reserved for artists residencies and studios.

🕙 1100–1900 (F–Sa), –1800 (Sun)
🏠 56 Artillery Ln., E1 7LS
📞 +44 (0)20 7377 4300
🌐 www.ravenrow.org

"I'm always impressed and educated to the point I try to make every show. Arrive from the Bishopsgate end and walk down the stunning old cobbled street."

– John Gilsenan, IWANT

21 Dennis Severs' House
Map C, P.105

Among the skyscrapers and business suits stands Dennis Severs' House, the mostly unlikely find in Spitalfields. Saved from demolition and intimately structured by the late Dennis Severs, a confirmed American Anglophile, this restored townhouse is what he called a "still-life drama". From the lighting to the mixtures and textures, each of the house's ten rooms was carefully set to relive the 18th-century world based on the era's paintings. For a more special experience, book a night visit when the house is lit by candles and filled with silence.

🕐 💲 Day visits: 1200–1400 (M), –1600 (Su), £10/5; Silent Night Tour: 1700–2100 (M, W, F), £15
🏠 18 Folgate St., E1 6BX
📞 +44 (0)20 7247 4013
URL www.dennissevershouse.co.uk

"This is no museum. It's a game to wander round and let yourself believe that the occupants have just left the room. Magical, in the truest sense of the word."
– Build

22 White Cubicle Toilet Gallery
Map I, P.109

Established by curator Pablo León de la Barra, the White Cubicle Toilet Gallery started out with an aim to host mini art exhibitions within the infamously tiny space of the ladies' toilet at the cult George and Dragon pub. Twenty years have gone by, and the gallery has followed its landlords to their new location, challenging artists to transform a humble space and engaging them as an antidote to London's commercial art scene. Past exhibitions have included the work of Prem Sahib, and art duo Tim Noble and Sue Webster.

🕐 Hours vary with programmes
🏠 The Queen Adelaide, 483 Hackney Rd., E2 9ED
📞 +44 (0)20 7012 1100　📘 @whitecubicle

"It's worth sneaking in!"
– Chrysostomos Naselos, Company

043

23 Hunterian Museum
Map C, P.104

Opened as a tribute to famed Scottish surgeon and anatomist, John Hunter (1728–93) best known for his research in dentistry and child development, Hunterian Museum is also a great place to spend the day drawing. With approximately 3,500 specimens and preparations from Hunter's collections, the museum displays many of his most famous specimens, including the skeleton of 'Irish Giant' Charles Byrne. You'll need to wear a special Museum Visitor security badge, which can be obtained at the College's Reception Desk.

🕐 1000–1700 (Tu-Sa)
🏠 1F, The Royal College of Surgeons of England, 35–43 Lincoln's Inn Fields, WC2A 3PE
📞 +44 (0)20 7869 6560
🔗 www.rcseng.ac.uk/museums/hunterian
🔖 The museum is due to reopen in 2020.

"It's full of jars of body parts and bone that are beautiful in a weird and wonderful way! Eat lunch before you go as you may not stomach it after!"
– Jane Bowler

24 Rio Cinema
Map G, P.108

Overlooking Dalston, this century-old sin-
gle-screened picturehouse has faced many
challenges to remain open. Rio's programme
offers a varied selection of mainstream
movies and art house releases, and the
cinema runs the annual Turkish and Kurdish
film festivals, midweek Classic Matinées
and participates in the Gay and Lesbian film
festival. Refurbished mindfully in 1999, much of
Rio's interior remains faithful to Frank Ernest
Bromige's 1930s Art Deco design.

S £9.50–11.50 (Tu–F after 1700, Sa & Su), £5–8.50
(Tu–F before 1700), £6–7 (M except P.H. Mondays)
A 107 Kingsland High St., E8 2PB
C +44 (0)20 7241 9410
URL riocinema.org.uk

*"Keep an eye on the special features.
Don't miss out on the delicious cakes."*

– brose-fogale

Markets & Shops

Local designs, international finds and street food

Markets in London are a great place to see a slice of London life. Originally emerging around the city to cater to local communities' daily needs, marketplaces today offer goods as varied as art and antiques, as well as fresh produce, daily catches, and all manner of clothing and sundries that attract a large population from outside town. Consequently these areas have seen new proliferations of street musicians, rare shops, cafés and restaurants congregate. Borough, Whitecross, Broadway, Brick Lane, Camden, Columbia Road (#36) and Portobello markets are all great markets to scour. At the same time, new markets continue to take shape on busy urban walkways, often becoming foodie destinations, and deriving initiatives like KERB (#33).

Competing for space on London's streets sit a scattered wealth of adorable boutiques and department stores that stock a world of fine products, books and designer handpicked cuts. Get ready for eye-opening discoveries in the markets and shops listed here. As ever, popular shopping district Covent Garden remains a high point. Sale seasons are most often found in January, with the best to be had straight after Christmas, and in mid-June for about a month.

Ponto
Graphic design collective

Ponto is an independent design studio founded and operated by Eurico Sá Fernandes and Mariana Lobão. Our practice is merged into three main areas – print, digital and research.

Ti Pi Tin
050

The Peanut Vendor
051

Isaac McHale
Chef, The Clove Club & Luca

I am a chef. I run The Clove Club with Daniel Willis and Johnny Smith and Luca in Clerkenwell.

Thereza Rowe
Illustrator

Born in Brazil and adopted by the UK, I embrace both of my cultural backgrounds. I love drawing and spend most days in my studio dreaming of magic umbrellas and fox parties.

Magma
Books
052

Jean Jullien
Graphic artist

I'm a 34-year-old French graphic artist living and working in London.

Liberty
055

Kate Sclater
Graphic designer, Hyperkit

I founded design studio Hyperkit with my husband Tim Balaam in 2001. Our studio's output includes branding, art direction and design for print, screen and physical space.

Pernilla Ohrstedt
Architect & designer

My studio works with projects ranging from buildings to exhibitions. With Asif Khan, I designed Coca-Cola's Beatbox pavilion, appearing at London Olympics 2012.

Orbital
Comics
054

Lamb's
Conduit
Street
056

Roger Whittlesea
Design manager, Proud Creative

Partner, design manager, producer, client wrangler and chief make-it-happener at multidisciplinary design company, Proud Creative.

Brixton Market 059

Gavin Lucas
Writer & editor

I've been a contributing editor to leading communication arts journal and CR blog for over ten years. I've authored books, been a headline DJ at Glastonbury, and run burger blog Burgerac.

Actress
Producer

Actress is the recording name of Darren Cunningham. His work draws on a deep appreciation for early 80s funk, electro and art rock. He has just released his fifth album, *AZD*.

Momosan Shop 058

KERB 060

Mark Bloom
Graphic designer, Mash Creative

I'm the founder of London-based graphic design studio Mash Creative, author of *14 Years / 41 Logos* and creator of the State of the Obvious merchandise range.

Spitalfields Market 062

Christopher Duffy
Furniture designer, Duffy London

I'm born, raised and running Duffy London. I live in Wapping by the Thames, my favourite part of London, and I'm lucky enough to be able to see the river from my windows.

Angus MacPherson
Graphic designer

I studied graphic design at Leeds College of Art and now live and work in East London. I trained for print design but I like to experiment with other mediums and disciplines.

Leather Lane Market 061

Columbia Road Flower Market 063

25 Ti Pi Tin
Map G, P.108

Originally an online platform established in 2009 by Katja Chernova, Ti Pi Tin is an ardent proponent of independent and self-publishing. Stocking a phenomenal range of limited edition books, small press monographs, journals and zines, each distinct for their themes and packaging, the shop also offers its space for a compelling lineup of talks, screenings and social gatherings for debates and discussions around contemporary independent art publishing. Ti Pi Tin stocks books from Café Royal Books, Karma, Nieves, Preston is my Paris Publishing and twelvebooks, among others.

🕐 1200–1900 (W–F), 1100–1800 (Sa), 1200–1800 (Su & by appointment)
🏠 47 Stoke Newington High St., N16 8EL   ✆ info@tipitin.com
URL www.tipitin.com

"A great place to dig into self-published books and magazines."

– Ponto

26 The Peanut Vendor
Map M, P.111

The Peanut Vendor's Becky and Barny share a long-term obsession with all that is old. Since deciding to turn their hobby into a full-time job, they travel the country and beyond to select the best in vintage furniture and design for their shop. From chairs to lighting, tables to posters, The Peanut Vendor collection combines the styles and designs of the early to mid-20th century with an affordable price tag. The duo also curated chairs and lighting for Shoreditch Town Hall bar and restaurant, The Clove Club.

🕐 0900–1730 daily
🏠 6 Gunmakers Ln., E3 5GG
📞 +44 (0)20 8981 8613
🌐 www.thepeanutvendor.co.uk

"Check out what they have online, and swing by to pick up some cool things for home."
– Isaac McHale, The Clove Club & Luca

27 Magma Books
Map B, P.103

Visual arts and graphic design books in unfussy surroundings continue to draw creative professionals and design enthusiasts to this longstanding independent retailer. Established in 2000 and envisioned by Brazilian Marc Valli and Spaniard Montse Ortuno as a clever place for creative retail, the winning platform has prospered with two branches and started their own magazine Elephant. Magma's flagship on Shorts Gardens features an event space and stocks design-led products and prints, including homeware and accessories by international designers and illustrators, often with short-runs and limited editions.

🕙 *Magma Clerkenwell: 1000-1900 (M-Sa)*
🏠 *117-119 Clerkenwell Rd., EC1R 5BY*
📞 *+44 (0)20 7242 9502*
🔗 *magma-shop.com*

"*Nearby the Covent Garden shop, London Graphic Centre is brilliant for good value art supplies. They have a business card board which you can pin yours in for free.*"
– Thereza Rowe

🕐 Magma Covent Garden (flagship): 1100–1900 (M–Sa), –1800 (Su)
🏠 29 Shorts Gardens, WC2H 9AP
📞 +44 (0)20 7240 7970

28 Orbital Comics

Map B, P.103

Orbital is a landmark of comic book culture in London, with much of its space dedicated to comics and anime, featuring a huge selection of translated titles, graphic novels, classic back-issues and merchandise bought from around the world, as well as independent works published by Orbital Small Press. Its gallery also hosts signing, forums and themed exhibitions regularly where comic enthusiasts get to meet the authors in person and pick up original artworks. The Orbiting Pod is where weekly reviews, commentary and interviews can be read or listened online.

🕐 1030–1900 (M–Tu, F–Sa), –1930 (W–Th), 1130–1700 (Su)
🏠 8 Great Newport St., WC2H 7JA
📞 +44 (0)20 7240 0591
🔗 www.orbitalcomics.com

"Their amazing wall of back issues is a real treat. I once saw a really old issue of Namor the Sub-Mariner whose cover was the most vivid red. A total print-gasm."

– Jean Jullien

29 Liberty
Map A, P.102

Liberty is a synonym for extravagance in a fashionable way. Standing on Great Marlborough Street and overlooking Carnaby Street at its back, the emporium, which sells everything from designer fashion and beauty to homewares and outdoor living, exemplifies high style with an eclectic mix of new brands and designer labels often well received by the industry. Beyond its long history of artistic collaborative projects with designers and brands, Liberty is now stretching its reach to provide sewing classes, grooming and tailoring services all within the walls of its fabulous four-storey Tudor building.

🕐 1000–2000 (M-Sa), 1130–1800 (Su, browsing only before noon)
🏠 Regent St., W1B 5AH
☎ +44 (0)20 7734 1234
URL libertylondon.com

"Be sure to visit the fabric department to see all the beautiful Liberty prints."
— Kate Sclater, Hyperkit

30 Lamb's Conduit Street
Map C, P.104

Find Lamb's Conduit on a quiet street in a leafy Bloomsbury neighbourhood. The area is a long-time home to artisans and independent shops, whose owners often organise open events and offer free glasses of wine. Stop by Folk and Oliver Spencer for unusual and exclusive apparel, Persephone Books, which publishes neglected fiction by mostly women writers, and designer Ben Pentreath's eponymous home accessories store, run with decorative artist Bridie Hall.

🏠 *Lamb's Conduit st., WC1*

1 & 2. Persephone Books
3 & 4. Folk

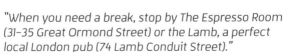

"*When you need a break, stop by The Espresso Room (31-35 Great Ormond Street) or the Lamb, a perfect local London pub (74 Lamb Conduit Street).*"

– Pernilla Ohrstedt

31 Momosan Shop

Map G, P.108

Tiny but full of interesting objects, Momosan Shop is a mini showcase of founder Momoko Mizutani's own experience of living in a foreign country. Cultures intersect in practical and imaginative ways – with artisanal homewares, accessories, toys, stationery and furniture found around the UK, Europe and Mizutani's home country, Japan. Don't forget to check her news too as she could be hitting the road soon.

🕐 1100–1800 (Th-Su & by appointment)
🏠 79a Wilton Way, E8 1BG
📞 +44 (0)20 7249 4989
🔗 momosanshop.com

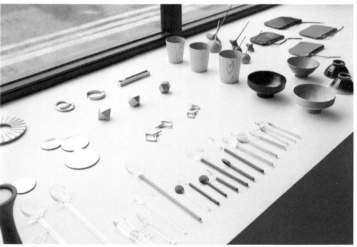

"Momoko has a great personality and good taste. Best buy: the archive boxes made to the same specification as those created for Stanley Kubrick."
– Roger Whittlesea, Proud Creative

32 Brixton Market

Map Q, P.111

Brixton is a close-knit community reflected in the huge and varied offering of products on offer in Brixton Street Market. Although the recently refurbished Brixton Village has risen to become a new London culinary and cultural destination with new cafés and live music, the road market remains vibrant and bursting with character, where traders engage customers and chitchat at leisure. Take Electric Avenue or Brixton Station Road to explore international goods, from Caribbean fruits to scented Malian charcoal, in the street market and find the arcade midway.

🕐 Road Market: 1000-1700 (F-Sa), Arcades: 0800-1800 (M), -2330 (Tu-Su) 🏠 Brixton Station Rd., SW9 8PA 🔗 brixtonmarket.net

"Brixton Village is also stuffed full of great places to eat – Fish, Wings and Tings, Franco Manca and Bukowski's to name a few."

– Actress

33 KERB
Map H, P.109

Born out of a love to engage with the community growing around street stalls, KERB is founded by ex-food hawker, Petra Barran, to transform humble curbside pavements into bustling foodie markets with a rotating mix of registered traders. kerbfood.com profiles the best stalls and vans, with regular updates about their locations. Each member has a knack for a particular cuisine, from family grills to organic salads, Asian fusion to all things British.

🕐 🏠 As of May 2017, regular locations include: Camden Market: 1100–1800 (M–Th), –1900 (F–Su); King's Cross: 1200–1400 (W–F); Gherkin: 1200–1400 (Th)
URL www.kerbfood.com

"Try a Cheeseburger at Mother Flipper, or a Heartbreaker burger at Tongue 'N Cheek."

– Gavin Lucas

34 Leather Lane Market

Map C, P.104

Hidden for more than 300 years in a back street between Clerkenwell Road and High Holborn, Leather lane weekday market trades much more than its name implies. A street full of pop-up food stalls selling food from around the world, the market is a Mecca for hungry office workers or those on the go. Mix your own lunch at bargain prices with Daddy Donkey's Burritos and Ptooch's veggie salad. A java from Department of Coffee or Prufrock makes for a good finish.

🕙 1000–1400 (M–F)
🏠 Leather Ln., EC1N 7T

"*Only open weekdays between 10am and 2pm. If going for food, expect long queues.*"

– Mark Bloom, Mash Creative

35 Spitalfields Market
Map C, P.105

Also known as Old Spitalfields Market, the former wholesale market now opens seven days
a week inside two Victorian halls. While the
Traders Market is a treasure trove of unique
finds for every taste and pocket, the Saturday
Style Market introduces original fashion and interior creations by local designers. Spitalfields
Arts Market offers affordable artworks from
March until Christmas. Allow at least an hour to
go around the market. There's street art, retro
shops and inspirations just about everywhere
you look.

🕐 1000-1700 (M-F), 1100- (Sa), 0900- (Su & P.H.)
Saturday Style Market: 1100-1700 (Sa)
🏠 Brushfield St., E1 6AA
📞 +44 (0)20 7377 1496
URL *www.spitalfields.co.uk*

*"I recommend walking up to Redchurch Street then
through to Curtain Road, where there are some
quirky design and clothing shops scattered around."*
– Christopher Duffy, Duffy London

36 Columbia Road Flower Market

Map F, P.107

Whether it's rain, shine, or Easter Sunday, this busy Sunday market is filled with locally-grown or globally-sourced cut flowers and plants, next to a brilliant selection of independent garden shops, boutiques, small galleries and cafés on both sides of the road. Get to the market early to beat the crowds, or late afternoon for some real bargains as the stall owners try and sell off their final bits of stock. Look for a great pub called the Royal Oak at No.73, which is a step back in time, and does a mean Sunday dinner (make sure you book!).

🕐 0800–1500 (Su)
🏠 Columbia Rd., E2 7RG
URL www.columbiaroad.info

> "The busy atmosphere can be fairly intense. Hit up some of the cafés and bars on Rivington Street, if you fancy a slightly lower paced bite to eat or drink."
>
> – Angus MacPherson

Restaurants & Cafés

Modern classics, ethnic food and exquisite cakes

Tea and jam do not conclude British cuisine. With Londoners more conscious of healthy eating and the environment, it is common to find restaurants and cafés in London that opt for organic or sustainable produce from local farmers or social enterprises, which they work like magic to produce memorable tastes imbued with British flair. If you're looking to exhilarate your taste buds, London offer a fantastic variety drawn from all around the world at every available price-tag. Almost every ethnic cuisine can be traced on its streets, counter-balanced with the English classics, from seafood shacks to afternoon teas to pub roasts. For an authentic taste of East End London, pie and mash with liquor (a vivid green parsley sauce) makes for cheap, filling comfort food, best from the notable F. Cooke (*9 Broadway Market, E8 4PH*) and Manzes (*76 High st., E17 7LD*). Fish 'n Chips are obviously a thing everyone visiting the UK should have at least once. The Rock & Sole Plaice in Covent Garden (*45-49 Endell St., WC2H 9AJ*) is a great place to go and in the summer you can sit outside and watch the world go by.

IS TROPICAL
Band

We make psychedelic-tinged pop music and have been travelling all over because of it. IS TROPICAL is signed to New York based independent label Axis Mundi.

Floyd's on Shacklewell Lane
068

David Wilson
Music video director

Best known for his music video work, David Wilson has created for acts such as Arctiv Monkeys and Tame Impala. He was a Grammy nominee in 2015 for video 'We Exist'.

Mildreds
071

E5 Bakehouse
069

Leif Podhajsky
Artist & creative director

My work explores the relevance of nature and psychedelic experience. Through these subjects I attempt to inspire viewers into realigning themselves with their surroundings.

L'atelier Dalston
072

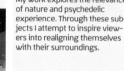

Jess Bonham
Photographer

I was born and bred in South London, now based in East London. Having lived here almost all my life, London remains my all-time favourite city. It has so much variety in so many forms.

Nuno Mendes
Chef, Taberna do Mercado

I am a soft-spoken and polite Portuguese traveller with a passion for food and people. At Taberna do Mercado, Antonio Galapito and I capture and reinterpret Portuguese flavours.

Koya Bar
070

Geoffrey J. Finch
Creative director, Blouse

Previously creative director at Topshop and Antipodium, I'm a Libran with Virgo rising and moon in Scorpio. I originally hail from rural Australia and created unisex fashion label, Blouse.

Elliot's Café
073

Krankbrother
DJ duo

We are Danny and Kieran Clancy, specialising in 'off location' electronic music. Our parties showcase artists in unique locations like rooftops, streets, beaches, and railway arches.

Skylon
077

Jim Sutherland
Founder, Studio Sutherl&

Formerly the co-founder of Hat-trick Design, Jim Sutherland set up Studio Sutherl& in 2014. His work spans across identities, stamps, books, and signs. He lives in, and loves, London.

Robert Ryan
Paper artist

Born in Cyprus, I studied Fine Art at Trent Polytechnic and the Royal College of Art, London, specialising in printmaking. Since 2002, I've turned to creating through paper cutting.

Bonnie
Gull
076

Sketch
078

Jonathon Jeffrey
Creative director, Bibliothèque

Founding partner of Bibliothèque who arrived in East London in 1996. I love design, art, film, food and shoes, and like to try to combine all of these into a weekend walk.

St. John
Bar &
Restaurant
082

S.E.H. Kelly
Fashion design collective

We are Sara Kelly and Paul Vincent, the founders of S.E.H. Kelly. Since 2009 we have made clothes in a workshop in East London with British mills and factories.

Andy Harvey
Design director, Moving Brands

A multidisciplinary design director, type nerd and Japan obsessive, I live in Walthamstow and have worked for Marque Creative, Burberry and Saturday.

LARDO
080

Bob Bob
Ricard
083

37 **Floyd's on Shacklewell Lane**
Map G, P.108

Model-turned-restaurateur Konrad Lindholm
has channelled his sensibilities for colour into
his little kitchen on Shacklewell Lane. Almost
editorial, most dishes fly in bright colours – like
sea bream fillet with golden crispy skin, set
against purple majestic potato salad, mange
tout, radishes and olive tapenade. Taste-wise,
it's a spectacular take on high cuisine with Eu-
ropean hints at modest prices. Seasonal flora
perks up the panelled interior, and are placed
on tables in recycled bottles.

🕐 *1200–1500 (M–F), 1100–1600, 1800–2330 (Th–Sa)*
🏠 *89 Shacklewell Ln., E8 2EB*
📞 *+44 (0)20 7923 7714*
📘 *@floydsonshacklewelllane*

"*Join a broke band in the local area to beg for free
coffees and (sometimes) succeed.* "
– IS TROPICAL

38 E5 Bakehouse
Map G, P.108

E5's bakers get busy crafting their beautiful breads inside a spruced up railway arch everyday before first light, and their sourdough pre-ferment has become the stuff of legend. Simple breakfasts and Greek-inspired fresh lunch menus are designed and prepared with organic ingredients and served daily, with authentic Italian sourdough pizzas on Sundays. The bakery also runs a one-day bread class, which typically covers the making of a French Sourdough, ciabatta, 66% rye and bagels.

Café: 0700-1900 daily,
Shop: 0800-1700 (M-W), -1800 (Th-Sa)
Arch 395, Mentmore Ter., E8 3PH
+44 (0)20 8986 9600
e5bakehouse.com

"Seriously the best place for food and vibe. The soups with fresh bread is soul nourishing. Get there early for lunch before all the goodness runs out."

– Leif Podhajsky

39 **Koya Bar**
Map B, P.103

At KOYA, which Nuno Mendes recommended in the first place, udon noodles were the star dish. Although the store closed its doors in 2015, its head chef Shuko Oda remains with Koya Bar, churning out breakfasts and noodles prepped with local ingredients and total Japanese technique. Enjoy the udon by itself, in hot broth or cold sauce, with up to 30 meat and vegetable combinations. A variety of small plates can be ordered as accompaniments, alongside imported beers, sake and Shochu. Check the boards to try the latest local seasonal specials.

🕐 0830-2230 (M-W), -2300 (Th-F), 0930-2300 (Sa), 0930-2200 (Su) 🏠 50 Frith St., W1D 4SG
🔗 www.koyabar.co.uk 🖋 Walk-ins only

"It's amazing how a Japanese chef cooks with local ingredients in a Japanese way. I like udon, but I always have their specials. I love the unpredictability."

– Nuno Mendes, Taberna do Mercado

40 Mildreds
Map A, P.102

Even for meat-eaters, Mildreds vegetarian menu is one of the best in town. Handpicking organic ingredients where possible and using a network of small businesses for their supplies, this friendly place serves a comprehensive drinks and cocktails list next to their internationally inspired vegetarian food made daily on the premises. Their salad bar means you can pick up something to take away and eat in a park on a summer's day.

🕐 1200–2300 (M–Sa)
🏠 45 Lexington St., W1F 9AN
📞 +44 (0)20 7494 1634
🔗 www.mildreds.co.uk
✒ Walk-ins only

"If you're planning to grab lunch (eat in or take away) get there EARLY (before 1pm) as seated spaces fill up fast and the best bits of the salad bar can go quickly."

– David Wilson

41 L'atelier Dalston
Map G, P.108

Founders of L'Atelier Ludo and Benjamin don't stop at producing fresh coffee, cakes and decent lunches. Featuring mishmash colour and mismatched ornaments, this little place doubles as a mart where furniture they collect from flea markets, travels and what others might term junk from the street are restored and put up for sale. Roadside seating and tables by large windows provide a perfect vantage point to overlook activities on Dalston's main street. Wine, cheese and cocktails replace the daytime menu after nightfall.

🕑 0800-1800 (M-F), 0900- (Sa-Su)
🏠 31 Stoke Newington Rd., N16 8BJ
📞 +44 (0)20 7254 3238
📘 @LatelierDalston

"It has a very calm and considered interior so is a good place to come and work quietly or have meetings. Eat Cake!"
– Jess Bonham

42 Elliot's Café
Map C, P.105

Sneak a peek at what's eye-catchingly good in Borough Market on your way to Elliot's for a hint of what their daily menu will offer. In the relaxed and convivial atmosphere of the market's unofficial café, chef and owner Brett Redman who co-runs The Richmond and Jidori in London delights with simple, seasonal ingredients cooked over a wood-fired grill, plentiful wild garlic and olive bread supplied daily alongside a list of biodynamic wines. Go for coffee, cheese and cured meat in between meals when the kitchen is closed.

🕐 1200–2200 (M–Sa)
🏠 12 Stoney St., SE1 9AD
📞 +44 (0)20 7403 7436
URL www.elliotscafe.com

"Get the tartare, the oysters, the mussels, whatever meat special is going, definitely the ice-cream, obviously the cheese. Actually, get as much as you possibly can."

– Geoffrey J. Finch, Blouse

Bonnie Gull

Map A, P.102

Born from the pop-up Seafood Shack in Hackney, and with the successes of other projects, Bonnie & Wild and Bonnie-on-Sky under their belts, Bonnie Gull excels in creating a whole eating experience. With quality catches fresh from the sea daily and irresistible modern presentations, most take a few seconds to admire the plate before diving in. Every fish, oyster and crab they offer are 100% responsibly sourced and British produced. Enjoy the reasonably priced menu designed by head chef, Christian Edwardson, who learnt his craft from Michelin-starred chef Pierre Koffmann.

🕐 *1200 till late daily* 🏠 *21A Foley St., W1W 6DS*
📞 *+44 (0)20 7436 0921* 🔗 *www.bonniegull.com*

"*It's a taste of the British seaside in the city. Sit outside and enjoy getting messy with a Devon Crab.*"

– krankbrother

44 Skylon
Map C, P.104

Taking its name from the now-demolished landmark structure built for the 1951 Festival of Britain, Skylon serves up modern British cuisine against a scenic backdrop of London's skyline and the Thames. Formerly of the acclaimed Savoy Grill and now Skylon's executive chef, Kim Woodward brings her wealth of culinary knowledge to this airy dining room, with casual grills and wonderful brunch to sate your savoury cravings. Those aiming for an original drink, stop by its centrepiece bar and let the occasional live music round out your day.

🕐 1200-0100 (M-F), 1130-0100 (Sa), -2230 (Su)
🏠 Royal Festival Hall, Belvedere Rd., SE1 8XX
📞 +44 (0)20 7654 7800
🔗 www.skylon-restaurant.co.uk

"Wonderful location, food and views over the Thames, especially at night."

– Jim Sutherland, Studio Sutherl&

45 Sketch
Map A, P.102

Housed in a Grade II listed townhouse whose former occupants included RIBA and Christian Dior, Sketch is a total sensory experience formulated by Morad Mazouz, with wildly imaginative dining rooms – from outlandish interiors and fittings to famous loo pods and curated playlists. And then there's the "New French" menu devised by head chef, Pierre Gagnaire, a loose adaption of the cuisine served at his three Michelin-starred restaurant in Paris. If dinner sounds ambitious, afternoon tea features classic items given imaginative twists and fine attention to detail.

🕐 0800–0200 (M–F), 1000– (Sa), 1000–0000 (Su)
🏠 9 Conduit St., W1S 2XG
📞 +44 (0)20 7659 4500
URL www.sketch.uk.com

"Go to the toilets, very interesting!"
– Robert Ryan

46 LARDO
Map G, P.108

Much of LARDO's soul comes from its charcuterie, which has been perfected using Mangalitza pigs. The curly-hair breed is specially bred in Hungary and raised in Somerset on fresh fruit and vegetables for 18 months, and the meat is hung for a week before being used to make pepperoni featured on pizza toppings and antipasti. Expect a modern British interpretation of the classic pizzeria. Naturally, all of LARDO's pasta and breads are made in house.

🕐 1100–2300 (M–Sa), –2200 (Su)
🏠 197–205 Richmond Rd., E8 3NJ
☎ +44 (0)20 8985 2683
URL www.lardo.co.uk

"LARDO is smart and informal.
Go for authentic pizza and great salads."
– Jonathon Jeffrey, Bibliothèque

47 St. John Bar & Restaurant
Map C, P.104

Fergus Henderson's pared-down nose-to-tail dining philosophy almost single-handedly re-established offal as eatable and brought British traditional cooking back into vogue. But St. John's is more than just a faddish fashion. Alongside the signature dishes, their menu is a daily work in progress with a range of meats, seafood and greens paired with French wines. Their bakery on Druid Street, famous for its fresh doughnuts, is well worth a trip.

🕐 1200–1500, 1800–2300 (M–F), 1800–2300 (Sa), 1230–1600 (Su), Bakery: 0900–1600 (Sa–Su)
🏠 26 St. John St., EC1M 4AY
📞 +44 (0)20 7251 0848
🔗 www.stjohngroup.uk.com

"Clever and honest British food in a fantastic old smokehouse. The bar is just as good to eat and drink in as the restaurant itself."
– S.E.H. Kelly

48 Bob Bob Ricard
Map A, P.102

Sink into one of Bob Bob Ricard's many royal-blue booths and soak up its Great Gatsby vibe celebrating classic Art Deco aesthetics. Heavily plated with gold and adorned with mirrors, terrazzo tiles, mahogany furnishings and intimate lighting, Bob Bob Ricard blends the romance of 20th-century train travel with a fine wine menu and upscale Russian and British comfort food. Book well in advance to avoid disappointment, and bash their trademark "press for champagne" button to fill fun.

🕐 1230-1500, 1800-0000 (Su-W), -0100 (Th-Sa)
🏠 1 Upper James St., W1F 9DF
📞 +44 (0)20 3145 1000
URL bobbobricard.com
🔗 12+

"A great take on comfort food. Check out the champagne service buttons on every table."

– Andy Harvey, Moving Brands

Nightlife

Live gigs, club nights and original cocktails

British music has impacted the world. Pop and rock flourished under bands like The Beatles and The Rolling Stones, and the country's huge ability to create, innovate and produce has birthed myriad new sounds and movements including Punk, Brit-pop, Madchester, Trip Hop, and particularly from London, Drum 'n' Bass and Dubstep. Sniff around and it's not too difficult to walk in the footsteps of these famous bands through their favourite haunts and hangouts. Meanwhile, budding new music and artists percolate and can reveal themselves anytime, anywhere – in tube stations, pubs, cafés and speakeasies – and are definitely worth keeping an ear out for. Music lovers will find live gigs and club nights seven days a week, in long established entertainment districts like Soho as well as venues at the top of Kingsland road between thriving hubs Dalston and Stoke Newington. For those who prefer to chill with a perfectly-crafted cocktail, seek out hidden bars like The Nightjar (#50) and ECC Chinatown (#51). Beer lovers, a bottle of Camden Hells Lager is a good keepsake, and revellers can get drunk gently at the nice pubs on the water's edge. But London can also mean more refined nighttimes. Some of the city's best performance art programmes can be found at Vogue Fabrics and Southbank Centre (#1), from where you could also walk between Westminster Bridge and the Millennium Bridge at night to view London in all its glory.

Owen Gildersleeve
Designer & illustrator

I'm an ADC Young Guns award winner and member of design collective, Evening Tweed. I enjoy experimenting with materials, as well as collaborating with stylists to bring ideas to life.

The Nightjar 089

Ian Stevenson
Artist

My work reflects the reality of living in the 21st Century, ranging from distorted characters to coffee cups. My influences are from my surroundings, everyday life and the TV.

Sam Bompas
Food artist, Bompas & Parr

A Cancerian who likes to imagine his bathroom being a neanderthal party grotto. I'm one half of Bompas & Parr who creates food art and make jelly.

Bethnal Green Working Men's Club 088

Oscar Diaz
Industrial designer

I work on projects for both cultural and commercial contexts. I studied fine art in Spain and industrial design at l'École des Beaux-Arts de Bordeaux and the Royal College of Art in London.

ECC Chinatown 092

The French House Soho 094

Tatty Devine
Jewellery design collective

Founded by Harriet Vine and Rosie Wolfenden, Tatty Devine designs and micro-manufactures original jewellery. Our designs are all about expressing oneself in a fun and distinctive way.

Marshmallow Laser Feast
Multimedia creative studio

Memo Akten, Robin McNicholas and Barney Steel. We love food, cocktails, parties and laser beams.

Union Chapel 093

Cafe OTO 095

Rosie Lee
Creative agency

We are a creative team of designers, strategists and production experts. We deliver campaigns and brand experiences for clients like Activision, Nike and Uniqlo.

Dalston Roof Park
097

Troika
Multimedia creative agency

We are Eva Rucki, Conny Freyer and Sebastien Noel. Our work explores the intersection of rational thought, observation and the changing nature of reality and human experience.

Amy Harris
Artist

I'm a freelance illustrator and artist based in Hackney. I love the music, arts, culture and unexpected experiences that London offers as a city – it's a raw and inspiring place to live!

Village Underground
096

The Gallery Café
098

Freddy Taylor
Graphic designer

Born in London, studied in Edinburgh, now living back in London. Currently an art director and designer working at Wieden + Kennedy London.

Duck & Waffle
100

Karl Maier
Graphic artist, Craig&Karl

One half of the trans-Atlantic design and illustration duo Craig & Karl.

Huntley Muir
Artist collective

We are Su Huntley and Donna Muir working as one with over 30 years of shared vision spanning digital imaging and stage design. Based in The Barbican, we travel and work extensively in Europe and America.

Birthdays
099

ZTH Cocktail Lounge
101

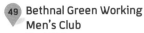

49 Bethnal Green Working Men's Club

Map I, P.109

A working men's social club till the 1970s, Bethnal Green Working Men's Club remains a traditional and fully functional East End hangout. The stage is lit with a massive red heart whose raunchy glow is matched with a curtain of streamers and ruby-hued carpet. An upstairs area stages new local artists, bands, DJs and performers. Some nights are also reserved for fantastically diverse events including 1940s swing nights, comedy evenings, cabaret and '90s style raves. Tickets required for selected events.

🕐 💲 *Hours & admission vary with events*
🏠 42–44 Pollard Row, E2 6NB
📞 +44 (0)20 7739 7170
🔗 www.workersplaytime.net
📎 18+ with photo ID

"Although events normally go on until the early hours, last entry is at 12. The bar is also cash only, so make sure to stop off at a cash point on your way."

– Owen Gildersleeve

- 🕐 1800–0100 (Su–W), –0200 (Th), –0300 (F–Sa)
- 💲 For music, per patron: £5 (W–Th & Su), £8 (F–Sa)
- 🏠 129 City Rd., EC1V 1JB
- 🔗 www.barnightjar.com
- 🖋 21+, online bookings recommended

50 The Nightjar
Map F, P.106

Like the bird of the same name, The Nightjar is completely camouflaged and awakes after dark. Hidden on City Road, behind the bar's understated doors lies an underground chamber, where live music ranging from blues and jazz to swing and bossa nova fills the room between 9.30–11.30pm. A strict no-standing policy is supposed to ensure the room is full but not overcrowded. Be prepared for surprises as all of The Nightjar's prohibition-themed or signature cocktails are precision-made and presented and raise the bar high. If The Nightjar is full, sink into Oriole, its sister in Farringdon, well-loved for precisely the same reasons.

"Retro cocktails in the bar are full of character. You will enjoy your cocktails! Book to avoid disappointment."

– Ian Stevenson

51 **ECC Chinatown**
Map B, P.103

Experimental Cocktail Club mixes extraordinary concoctions and sours, using strange yet supreme spirits, spices and juices in the most daring and unpredictable ways. With its root in Paris, its British edition is a three-floor prohibition-style speakeasy concealed by an ordinary worn backdoor in the depth of Chinatown. Although the club reserves room (including standing space) for walk-in customers, the doorman has a say in whether or not you're entering the club. Increase your chances for weekdays with email reservations before 5pm.

🕐 1800-0300 (M-Sa), -0000 (Su)
💲 £5 door charge after 11pm
🏠 13A Gerrard st., W1D 5PS
🔗 www.chinatownecc.com

"ECC makes the most grown-up cocktails in town. No 'mixology' frippery. Just sensational flavours that make you order five more cocktails."

– Sam Bompas, Bompas & Parr

52 Union Chapel
Map E, P.106

It is not often that you can listen to contemporary music in a shining example of Victorian Gothic architecture like the Union Chapel. The musical styles on offer are broad, with artists like Björk, Noel Gallagher and U2 having played in the past. Regular programmes include free Saturday lunchtime concerts (noon to 2pm) and a donation of £5 is invited towards the operation of free shows. The chapel runs a café at all concerts as part of their Margins Project for the homeless.

🕐 💲 Showtime & price vary with events
🏠 Compton Ter., N1 2UN
📞 +44 (0)20 7226 1686
🌐 www.unionchapel.org.uk
🎟 Tickets available from ticket agencies only

"Book in advance on the website.
Some events are free."

– Oscar Diaz

53 The French House Soho

Map B, P.103

Also known as "The French" among its loyal clientele, The French House is an iconic Soho watering hole albeit never a traditional one. It was once the meeting place of the Free French Forces organisation during WWII, and has long been a bohemian haunt and occasional exhibition space for Soho photographers. Good for small groups who don't mind standing in the often crowded room or out on the street. House lager is only served in halves, but order a French notable with a Breton Cider or Ricard.

🕐 1200–2300 (M-Sa), –2230 (Su)
🏠 49 Dean St., W1D 5BG
📞 +44 (0)20 7437 2477
🔗 frenchhousesoho.com

"One of the best pubs in Soho and full of characters. Turn off your mobile phone – it's not allowed in there!"

– Tatty Devine

54 Cafe OTO
Map G, P.108

The O2 may be the appointed destination for big names, but Cafe OTO is a venue for people who dare to try something different. Located on Ashwin Street near the Dalston Junction station, this cafe offers homemade cakes, Japanese snacks and a spread of single malt whiskies during the day, and a stage for the best in new music at night. Past performers include Keiji Haino, Kath Bloom, Sun Ra Arkestra and Yoshihide Otomo, to name a few. A subdivision, OTOProjects, opened on the same street in 2013, and stages workshops, talks, screenings and installations.

🕐 0830-1700 (M-F), 0930- (Sa), 1030- (Su)
🏠 18-22 Ashwin St., E8 3DL
🌐 www.cafeoto.co.uk
✐ Closes at 5pm on days with events

"Book tickets early as they often run out fast."

– Marshmallow Laser Feast

55 **Village Underground**
Map F, P.107

Inside this heritage-grade former coal store houses an epic art and gig venue praised for hosting some of the best in electronic music in London. Now, 20 years on, its programme continues to go from strength to strength, bringing the likes of Sophie aka Samuel Long and BBC Sound Of winner Ray BLK to the well-trodden stage. But that's not all. Keep abreast of its eclectic roll as tickets to their one-day shows go fast. Its changing mural and tube carriage co-working studios are also part of its charm.

🕐Ⓢ *Showtime & price vary with event*
🏠 *54 Holywell Ln., EC2A 3PQ*
☎ *+44 (0) 20 7422 7505*
🔗 *villageunderground.co.uk*
✐ *18+ (club/event), 16+ to 18 with adult (event)*

"Check what gigs are on before you visit and book – there's a lot of different nights on and events sell out frequently."

– Rosie Lee

56 Dalston Roof Park
Map G, P.108

Newly refurbished for 2017, Dalston Roof Park was opened by social enterprise, Bootstrap Company in 2010 as a summer venue for cultural exchange. Since then, it has evolved into an even more exciting venue for performances, film screenings and collaborations like 2013's Dazed On The Roof, which featured design talks and demonstrations co-organised with fashion magazine DAZED & CONFUSED. Show up early to the top of the Victorian print house and bag a seat on their massive mattresses or bean bags and enjoy outdoor cinema, accompanied by street food, lush gardens and London's skyline.

🕐 0900–1500, 1700–2300 (M–F), 1500–2345 (Sa),
1500–2200 (Su) 💲 £3
🏠 18 Ashwin St., E8 3DL 📞 +44 (0)20 7275 0825
📘 @dalstonroofparklondon

"Go for outdoor cinema and BBQ in the summer."

– Troika

57 **The Gallery Café**
Map I, P.109

Just a stone's throw from the Museum of Childhood (#18) in Bethnal Green, this non-profit vegetarian and vegan café is run by community charity, St. Margaret's House Settlement. With focus on the local population, the social hub arranges a diverse listing of affordable live music (from folk to blues), open mic nights, and a free Sunday cinema club that caters for myriad tastes. The Gallery Café also lives up to its name by holding monthly art exhibitions as part of First Thursdays organised by Whitechapel Gallery.

🕐 0800-2100 (M-F), 0900- (Sa), 0900-1900 (Su)
🏠 21 Old Ford Rd., E2 9PL
☎ +44 (0)20 8980 2092
📘 @thegallerycafelondon
🖉 Kitchen closes at 5pm

"Go to one of the music nights. They have a chapel in the garden with lovely acoustics! By day it's a good place for yummy lunch too."
– Amy Harris

58 Birthdays
Map G, P.108

No more complaints about the sound quality for indie music venues. Tucked into the foundation of an ordinary-looking residential block, Birthdays is an independent bar and venue with Max's Sandwich Shop filling out the ground-floor, and rave music taking over the live room down in the basement with a Funktion-one sound system. Since 2012, the club has collaborated with radio stations and independent music labels to throw parties, gigs and shows, introducing artists and groups from London and beyond.

🕐 1700-0000 (M-Th), -0300 (F), 1400-0300 (Sa), 1400-0000 (Su)
🏠 33-35 Stoke Newington Rd., N16 8BJ
📞 hello@birthdaysdalston.com
🔗 birthdaysdalston.com 📎 18+

"Because of House of Trax! Don't try and draw the stamp on your wrist, they'll catch ya."

– Freddy Taylor

 59 Duck & Waffle
Map C, P.105

Take a private lift and shoot up to the 40th
floor in 40 seconds for any meal you're feeling
at any hour. Quickly cemented as a London
classic since its opening, the restaurant offers
a breathtaking view over the Thames with
expertly prepared British cuisine. Imagine
yourself sitting in a comfy booth, munching on
some appetising crispy pig ear while watching
the sun rise over London Town. Their eponymous dish featuring crispy duck leg, runny
duck egg on waffle and maple syrup as crafted
by award winning Chef Dan Doherty is a great
way to soak up the excess of the night.

🕐 *24 hours*
🏠 *Heron Tower, 110 Bishopsgate, EC2N 4AY*
📞 *+44 (0)20 3640 7310*
URL *duckandwaffle.com*

 *"Tell the doorman downstairs you have a reservation,
even if you don't – it speeds things up."*

– Karl Maier, Craig&Karl

60 ZTH Cocktail Lounge

Map C, P.104

Inside this beautifully refurbished Georgian Townhouse finds this suave cocktail lounge with an eclectic interior and an equally eclectic mix of people to match. Very much like a living room inside a great aunt's house (which is a 13-room hotel) but with cocktail titan Tony Conigliaro to spice up the drink menu and an obsessive antique collection brimming every room, this place is a popular stamping ground for locals to sip and chat through the night. The house cocktails and the Conigliaro list will give away a piece of Clerkenwell's history and the imagery house owner's story.

🕐 0700-0000 (Su-W), -0100 (Th-Sa)
🏠 49-50 St John's Sq., EC1V 4JJ
📞 +44 (0)20 7324 4545
🔗 thezettertownhouse.com/clerkenwell/bar

"Open till late, table tennis downstairs.
Also good for Sunday brunch."

– Huntley Muir

MAP A

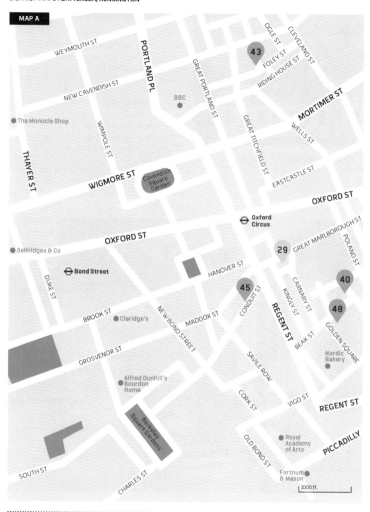

- 29_Liberty
- 40_Mildreds
- 43_Bonnie Gull
- 45_Sketch
- 48_Bob Bob Ricard

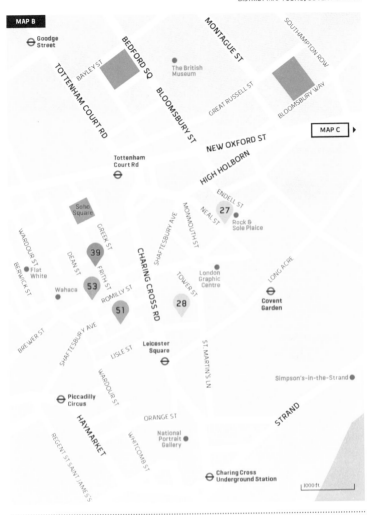

MAP B

Goodge Street

TOTTENHAM COURT RD

BAYLEY ST

BEDFORD SQ

MONTAGUE ST

SOUTHAMPTON ROW

The British Museum

BLOOMSBURY ST

GREAT RUSSELL ST

BLOOMSBURY WAY

MAP C ▶

NEW OXFORD ST

HIGH HOLBORN

Tottenham Court Rd

ENDELL ST

Soho Square

GREEK ST

SHAFTESBURY AVE

MOMMOUTH ST

NEAL ST

27

Rock & Sole Place

WARDOUR ST

DEAN ST

FRITH ST

39

CHARING CROSS RD

TOWER ST

London Graphic Centre

LONG ACRE

BERWICK ST

Flat White

Covent Garden

Wahaca

53

ROMILLY ST

28

51

BREWER ST

SHAFTESBURY AVE

LISLE ST

Leicester Square

ST MARTIN'S LN

Simpson's-in-the-Strand

WARDOUR ST

Piccadilly Circus

ORANGE ST

STRAND

HAYMARKET

REGENT ST SAINT JAMES'S

WHITCOMB ST

National Portrait Gallery

Charing Cross Underground Station

| 1000 ft.

○ 27_Magma Books

○ 28_Orbital Comics

● 39_Koya Bar

● 51_ECC Chinatown

○ 53_The French House Soho

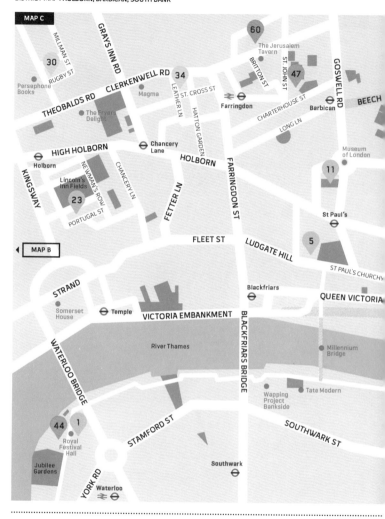

MAP C

MAP B

- 1_Southbank Centre
- 5_St. Paul's Cathedral
- 11_Postman's Park
- 23_Hunterian Museum
- 30_Lamb's Conduit Street
- 34_Leather Lane Market
- 44_Skylon
- 47_St. John Bar & Restaurant
- 60_Zetter Townhouse

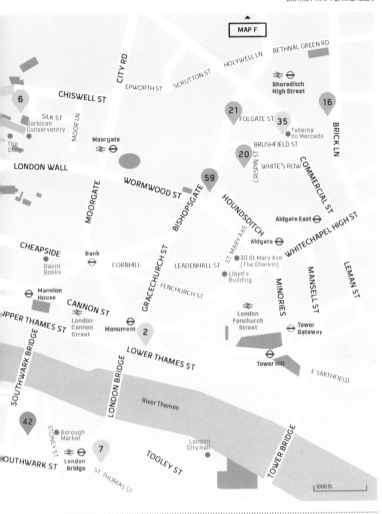

- 2_The Monument
- 6_The Barbican
- 7_The Shard
- 16_The Old Truman Brewery
- 20_Raven Row
- 21_Dennis Severs' House
- 35_Spitalfields Market
- 42_Elliot's Café
- 59_Duck and Waffle

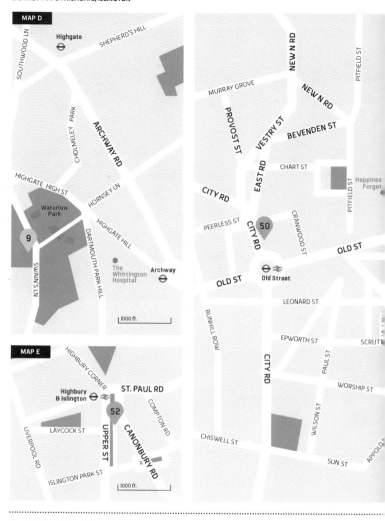

- 9_Highgate Cemetery
- 50_The Nightjar
- 52_Union Chapel

- 13..Kate MacGarry
- 36..Columbia Road Flower Market
- 55..Village Underground

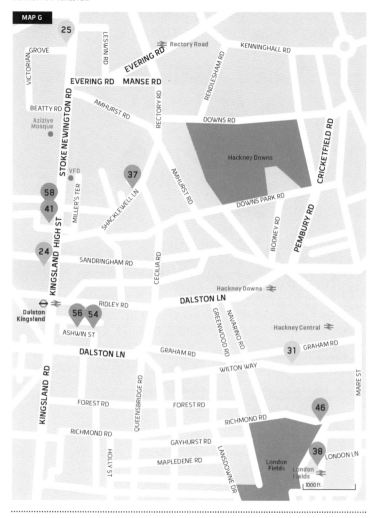

- 24_Rio Cinema
- 25_Ti Pi Tin
- 31_Momosan Shop
- 37_Floyd's on Shacklewell Lane
- 38_E5 Bakehouse
- 41_L'atelier Dalston
- 46_LARDO
- 54_Cafe OTO
- 56_Dalston Roof Park
- 58_Birthdays

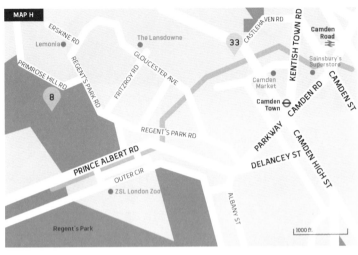

MAP H

MAP I

- 8. Primrose Hill
- 18. V&A Museum of Childhood
- 22. White Cubicle Toilet Gallery
- 33. KERB
- 49. Bethnal Green Working Men's Club
- 57. The Gallery Café

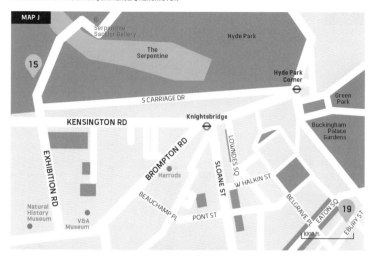

MAP J

Serpentine Sackler Gallery

Hyde Park

The Serpentine

15

Hyde Park Corner

S CARRIAGE DR

Green Park

KENSINGTON RD

Knightsbridge

Buckingham Palace Gardens

BROMPTON RD

LOWNDES SQ

EXHIBITION RD

Harrods

SLOANE ST

W HALKIN ST

BEAUCHAMP PL

BELGRAVE PL

EATON SQ

Natural History Museum

V&A Museum

PONT ST

19

EBURY ST

1000 ft.

MAP K

River Thames

CHELSEA BRIDGE RD

Grosvenor Bridge

3

CRINGLE ST

BATTERSEA PARK RD

PRINCE OF WALES DR

KIRTLING ST

SLEAFORD ST

QUEENSTOWN RD

Battersea Park

ASCALON ST

THESSALY RD

STEWART'S RD

1000 ft.

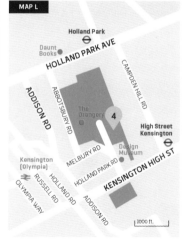

MAP L

Holland Park

Daunt Books

HOLLAND PARK AVE

CAMPDEN HILL RD

ADDISON RD

ABBOTSBURY RD

The Orangery

4

High Street Kensington

MELBURY RD

Design Museum

Kensington (Olympia)

HOLLAND PARK RD

KENSINGTON HIGH ST

RUSSELL RD

HOLLAND RD

OLYMPIA WAY

ADDISON RD

1000 ft.

....

- 3_Battersea Power Station
- 4_Holland Park
- 15_Serpentine Galleries
- 19_SHOWstudio

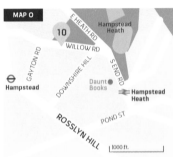

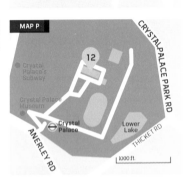

- 10_The Goldfinger House
- 12_The Crystal Palace Dinosaurs
- 14_Horniman Museum & Gardens
- 17_Bold Tendencies
- 26_The Peanut Vendor
- 32_Bixton Market

Accommodation

Hip hostels, fully-equipped apartments & swanky hotels

No journey is perfect without a good night's sleep to recharge. Whether you're backpacking or on a business trip, our picks combine top quality and convenience, whatever your budget.

 < £50 £51–200 £201+

The Ampersand Hotel

On the doorstep of V&A, the Natural History Museum and Hyde Park, the sleek newish Ampersand houses 111 modern, individually-styled rooms, a ground floor patisserie and small basement restaurant, which serves small plates to share, tapas-style. The gym offers personal trainers on request.

🏠 10 Harrington rd., SW7 3ER
📞 +44 (0)20 75 89 58 95
URL www.ampersandhotel.com

Shoreditch House, East London

Occupying the top floors of a renovated 1930s factory building, Shoreditch House is a hub for the local creative industries with rooftop pool, restaurant and gym. Vintage-themed rooms are small but bathrooms are stocked with Cowshed's no-animal-tested products.

🏠 Ebor st., E1 6AW
📞 +44 (0)20 77 39 50 40
URL www.shoreditchhouse.com

40 WiNKS

Originally used for fashion shoots and filming, interior designer David Carter's home is an 18th century Queen Anne townhouse and a glamorous alternative much loved by the fashion and Hollywood crowd. With only two guest rooms, this place aspires to offer a "home from home."

🏠 *109 Mile End rd., E1 4UJ*
📞 *+44 (0)20 77 90 02 59*
URL *www.40winks.org*

Clink78

🏠 78 King's Cross rd., WC1X 9QG
☎ +44 (0)20 34 75 30 00
URL www.clinkhostels.com

Bulgari Hotel London

🏠 171 Knightsbridge, SW7 1DW
☎ +44 (0)20 71 51 10 10
URL www.bulgarihotels.com/london

The Hoxton Shoreditch

🏠 *81 Great Eastern St., EC2A 3HU*
📞 *+44 (0)20 7550 1000*
🔗 *thehoxton.com*

The Ned

🏠 *27 Poultry, EC2R 8AJ*
📞 *+44 (0)20 3828 2000*
🔗 *www.thened.com*

Notes

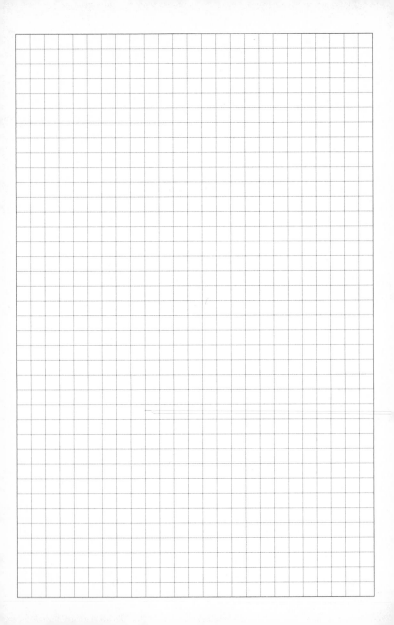

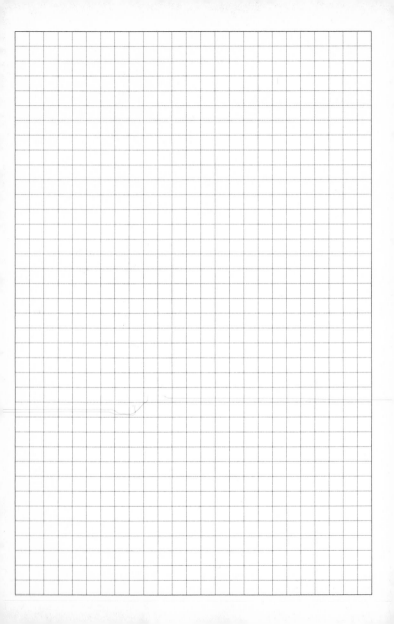

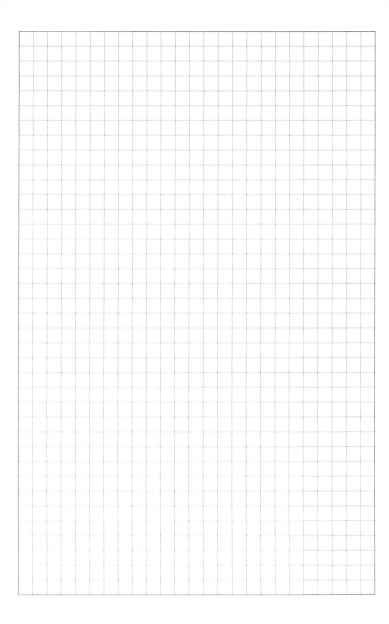

Index

Roger Whittlesea
@Proud Creative, *p058*
proudcreative.com

Sawdust, *p036*
madebysawdust.co.uk

Supermundane
aka Rob Lowe, *p027*
www.supermundane.com

Industrial

brose-fogale, *p045*
brosefogale.co.uk
Portrait by James Harris

Christopher Duffy
@Duffy London, *p062*
www.duffylondon.com

Oscar Diaz, *p093*
www.oscar-diaz.net

Multimedia

Marshmallow Laser Feast,
p095
www.marshmallowlaserfeast.
com

tokyoplastic, *p016*
www.tokyoplastic.com

Troika, *p097*
www.troika.uk.com

Music

Actress, *p059*
www.werkdiscs.com

IS TROPICAL, *p068*
istropical.com

Krankbrother, *p076*
www.krankbrother.com

Photography

Dan Tobin Smith, *p026*
www.dantobinsmith.com

Jess Bonham, *p072*
www.jessbonham.co.uk

Madame Peripetie, *p034*
www.madameperipetie.com

Nick Knight
@SHOWstudio, *p040*
www.showstudio.com
Portrait by Ruth Hogben

Publishing

Gavin Lucas, *p060*
burgerac.com
Portrait illustration by Roo
Walton

Photo & other credits

Battersea Power Station, *p016*
(Small) Battersea Power Station

Bob Bob Ricard, *p083*
(All) Bob Bob Ricard

Dennis Severs' House, *p042*
(All) Dennis Severs' House, Roelof
Bakker

Duck & Waffle, *p100*
(All) Duck & Waffle (middle) Dan
Doherty & Tom Cenci

ECC Chinatown, *p092*
(Interior, drinks) ECC Chinatown

Highgate Cemetery, *p024*
(All) Highgate Cemetery

Kate MacGarry, *p032*
(All) Kate MacGarry (top &
middle) Group Show - 'Don't
Worry', Olaf Breuning, FOS,
Dan McCarthy, Peter McDonald,
Muller van Severen (bottom)
SAMSON KAMBALU Capsules,
Mountains and Forts

Magma Books, *p052–053*
(All) Magma Books

Momosan Shop, *p058*
(All) Takanori Okuwaki

SHOWstudio, *p040*
(All) SHOWstudio

Sketch, *p078*
(Interiors) Sketch

Skylon, *p077*
(All) Skylon

Southbank Centre, *p014*
(All) Southbank Centre (top)
Morley von Sternberg (bottom)
Belinda Lawley

St. Paul's Cathedral, *p018*
(Façade) Graham Lacdao

St. John Restaurant &
Bar, *p082*
(Interior) St. John Restaurant
& Bar

The Barbican, *p019*
(Signage) Tom Flynn

The Gallery Café, *p098*
(Event) The Gallery Café

The Nightjar, *p089–091*
(Interior & musicians) Paul Storrie
(Cocktails) Dan Malpass

The Old Truman Brewery, *p036*
(Exterior) Alison Southwardn

The Peanut Vendor, *p051*
(Stock) The Peanut Vendor

The Shard, *p022*
(View) The View from The Shard

V&A Museum of
Childhood, *p028, 038–039*
(All) Victoria and Albert Museum,
London

Village Underground, *p096*
(All) Village Underground (Top)
Life Drawing by Dan Whiteson
(middle) Cat and Mouse - theatre
scratch performance by Matt
Humphrey (bottom) Superstition
by Luca Crescenzi

White Cubicle Toilet
Gallery, *p043*
(All) White Cubicle Toilet Gallery

ZTH Cocktail Lounge, *p101*
(All) ZTH Cocktail Lounge
-
In Accommodation: all courtesy
of respective hotels

CITIX60

CITIx60: London

Published and distributed by
viction workshop ltd

viction:ary™

7C Seabright Plaza, 9-23 Shell Street,
North Point, Hong Kong

Url: www.victionary.com
Email: we@victionary.com
🄵 @victionworkshop
🅥 @victionary_
🄾 @victionworkshop

Edited and produced by viction:ary

Concept & art direction: Victor Cheung
Research & editorial: Queenie Ho, Caroline Kong
Project Coordination: Katherine Wong, Jovan Lip
Design & map illustration: Bryan Leung, Cherie Yip, Beryl Kwan

Editing: Elle Kwan
Cover map illustration: David Ryan Robinson
Count to 10 illustrations: Guillaume Kashima aka Funny Fun
Photography: Gerard Puigmal

© 2014 – 2018 viction workshop ltd

Content is compiled based on facts available as of December 2017.
Travellers are advised to check for updates from respective locations
before your visit.

Seventh edition
ISBN 978-988-78500-8-3
Printed and bound in China

Acknowledgements

A special thank you to all creatives, photographer(s), editor, producers,
companies and organisations for your crucial contributions to our
inspiration and knowledge necessary for the creation of this book. And,
to the many whose names are not credited but have participated in the
completion of the book, we thank you for your input and continuous
support all along.

CITIX60

City Guides

CITIx60 is a handpicked list of hot spots that illustrates the spirit of the world's most exhilarating design hubs. From what you see to where you stay, this city guide series leads you to experience the best – places that only passionate insiders know and go.

Each volume is a unique collaboration with local creatives from selected cities. Known for their accomplishments in fields as varied as advertising, architecture and graphics, fashion, industry and food, music and publishing, these locals are at the cutting edge of what's on and when. Whether it's a one-day stopover or a longer trip, **CITIx60** is your inspirational guide.

Stay tuned for new editions.

Featured cities:

Amsterdam
Barcelona
Berlin
Copenhagen
Hong Kong
Istanbul
Lisbon
London
Los Angeles
Melbourne
Milan
New York
Paris
Portland
Singapore
Stockholm
Taipei
Tokyo
Vancouver
Vienna